·GOOD·
VEGETARIAN
·FOOD·FOR·
CHILDREN

·GOOD·
VEGETARIAN
·FOOD·FOR·
CHILDREN

JOHN COVENEY
&
RHONDA MOONEY

ANGUS
& ROBERTSON
PUBLISHERS

ANGUS & ROBERTSON PUBLISHERS

Unit 4, Eden Park, 31 Waterloo Road,
North Ryde, NSW, Australia 2113, and
16 Golden Square, London W1R 4BN,
United Kingdom

First published in Australia
by Angus & Robertson Publishers in 1987
First published in the United Kingdom
by Angus & Robertson UK in 1987

National Library of Australia
Cataloguing-in-publication data.

Coveney, John, 1950– .
  Good vegetarian food for children.

  Bibliography.
  Includes index.
  ISBN 0 207 15256 X.

  1. Vegetarian cookery.   2. Children — Nutrition.
  3. Cookery (Baby foods).   I. Mooney, Rhonda, 1963–
  II. Title.

641.5'636

Typeset by Graphicraft Typesetters Ltd, Hong Kong
Printed in Singapore

Illustrated by Alison Windmill

This book is dedicated to those parents
who want to feed their children (and themselves)
safe vegetarian diets.

FOREWORD

As the authors point out in the introduction to this book, many people follow vegetarian or semi-vegetarian diets for a variety of reasons. Some of these people enjoy a nutritious diet as part of a healthy lifestyle, but others place their health at risk because their diet does not provide the variety of foods necessary to support good health.

In extreme cases, vegetarianism is associated with dangerous fads such as the macrobiotic diet.

When the family diet is inadequate or marginal, the infants and children are the first to suffer because their nutritional needs are relatively high to provide for their growth and development. Food and nutrition are central to the physical and mental development, as well as the psychological and social development, of children.

In this book the authors have combined interesting background information and useful suggestions about planning family meals with a wide selection of nutritious recipes.

The authors, John Coveney, a dietitian, and Rhonda Mooney, a home economist, have combined their skills to produce this attractive and practical book which will be welcomed by parents, teachers and health workers.

Josephine F. Rogers
A.M., B.Sc., M.D.A.A.
National Chairperson
Australian Nutrition Foundation

CONTENTS

Section one
GENERAL INFORMATION

Section two
RECIPES

ACKNOWLEDGMENTS

We are grateful to the staff of the Department of Nutrition and Dietetics of the Children's Hospital, Sydney, who helped improve the recipes and the information in this book. Special mention must go to Sue Thompson, Chief Dietitian, without whose help this venture would never have begun.

Many thanks to Rose Borg for typing and to Melanie Harris for help and encouragement.

John Coveney, B.Sc. (Hons) Nutr., M.H.P.Ed., M.D.A.A.
Rhonda Mooney, Cert. Home Econ.

INTRODUCTION

You don't have to be a food crank or faddist to be a vegetarian today. Many people now follow total or semi-vegetarian lifestyles. And they are much healthier for it. In fact, surveys of vegetarian groups like the Seventh Day Adventists have shown that they have less heart disease, obesity and high blood pressure than the rest of the population. This is a tremendous advantage nowadays as these conditions are widespread and are serious health risks.

We have written this book for parents who want to feed their children vegetarian diets. It is divided into two sections.

Section one contains useful information on vegetarian diets. Here you will learn about properly planning vegetarian meals for children.

Section two provides some excellent recipes for children as well as the whole family. All recipes have been thoroughly tested. Most include dairy products or eggs because the nutritional needs of vegetarian children are easier to meet if these foods are included in their diet.

WEIGHTS
AND MEASURES

The following abbreviations are used throughout this book:

mcg = microgram

mg = milligram

g   = gram

kg = kilogram

mm = millimetre

cm = centimetre

mL = millilitre

L   = litre

All amounts conform to standard metric cup and spoon measurements.
Please note that:

1 metric cup = 250 mL

1 tablespoon = 20 mL

1 teaspoon   = 5 mL

Spoon measures are *level* spoonfuls.

Section one
GENERAL
INFORMATION

WHO ARE VEGETARIANS?

Throughout history there have always been those who have preferred not to eat meat. However, the term "vegetarian" was first recorded around the middle of the nineteenth century. Before this vegetarians were known as Pythagoreans — perhaps we should have called this book "Feeding Small Pythagoreans"!

The common theme of vegetarianism is the avoidance of flesh. But within the scope of the vegetarian diet are a whole range of options, explained in detail below.

LACTO-VEGETARIAN
The diet consists of plant foods, e.g. fruits, vegetables, grains and legumes (beans, peas and lentils). These are complemented with milk and milk products, e.g. cheese and yoghurt.

LACTO-OVO-VEGETARIAN
Here again the diet consists of all plant foods plus milk and milk products, but also includes eggs.

VEGAN (often called strict or pure vegetarians)
The diet consists only of plant foods. All foods of animal origin, including milk, cheese and eggs, are excluded.

FRUITARIAN
The diet consists only of plant foods but concentrates on those that do not involve destruction of the plant, e.g. fruits and nuts. Foods are usually eaten raw. This diet is unsuitable during pregnancy or for children.

MACROBIOTIC

The diet involves a progression through various levels of food restriction. Early stages allow consumption of meat, but during later stages the variety of foods becomes very narrow. Advanced stages of the diet cannot provide the nourishment that children need.

Since a balanced vegetarian diet is now recognised as being very healthful, a large number of people classify themselves as semi-vegetarian and only eat meat, chicken or fish on special occasions and at social events. But an important question for many parents is: Can my child be safely fed a vegetarian diet?

The short answer is yes. However, the diet needs to be well planned if it is to meet the nutritional demands of a growing child. Diets that do not contain any animal products (milk, cheese, eggs etc.), like Vegan, require extra-special attention. The liberal use of a fortified soya milk (see page 7) is strongly recommended. Fruitarian, macrobiotic and other fad diets cannot provide enough necessary nourishment for growing children or pregnant women. These diets are potentially dangerous and are strongly discouraged.

FEEDING
VEGETARIAN INFANTS

BEFORE BIRTH

A child's need for good food starts long before birth. Babies in the womb require the correct balance of nutrients if they are to grow and develop properly. Throughout pregnancy, vegetarians should make sure that they have an adequate diet for themselves and their babies. Remember that the nutritional needs of all women are increased during pregnancy. For vegetarians the nutrients requiring special attention are calcium, vitamin B_{12} and iron.

An extra 500 mg of calcium are needed every day after the first 12 weeks of pregnancy. This amount can easily be obtained from dairy foods. Vitamin B_{12} is also found in dairy foods (except yoghurt) and eggs. You will need about 4 mcg of vitamin B_{12} each day. Iron can be tricky. Wholegrain cereals, iron-fortified breakfast cereals, dried beans, peas and lentils and leafy green vegetables are your best bet. You will need about 15 mg of iron every day after the first 12 weeks of pregnancy. A useful way of meeting the extra needs of pregnancy is to use a fortified soya milk (see page 7). These "milks" are made for infants but are fine for adults, too, and make good soya shakes and custards. The tips given later in this book about including iron, calcium and vitamin B_{12} in the diets of vegetarian children are also relevant to pregnant vegetarians.

Important note

Mushrooms, vegetables, Spirulina (a kind of plankton), yeast, comfrey (a herb), fresh goat's milk and seaweed are often promoted as good sources of vitamin B_{12} for vegetarian mothers. This is not true. The vitamin content of these foods is often very low and quite unpredictable. Many cases of deficiency have been reported in mothers and babies who have relied on food with dubious vitamin contents. Proprietary vitamin supplements are cheap and easy to buy — and they are a far safer bet.

THE EARLY DAYS

Up to the age of 4 to 5 months mother's milk is the most important food for all babies. This will provide all the nourishment babies need. Breast milk is especially good because:

- the nutrients in breast milk are very well absorbed by the baby
- during a feed the composition of breast milk changes to meet the needs of the infant
- it is sterile and clean
- it helps to protect the baby against infection
- allergy to breast milk is extremely rare.

Women who breast feed usually miss their monthly periods. Since iron is lost during menstrual bleeding, breast feeding is a real advantage, especially for vegetarian mums.

Vegetarians who are breast feeding need to ensure that their diets are adequate. Earlier advice on an adequate diet during pregnancy also applies to lactation. Breast feeding also demands extra energy (kilojoules). If sufficient weight is gained during pregnancy (about 10–12 kg), the extra energy needed during lactation will be met by the fat stored in the body. However, lactating women should ensure that their food intake is kept high. Breast milk supplies may suffer in quantity and quality if enough kilojoules are not eaten.

Infant formulae are available for mothers who are unable to breast feed. There are many varieties on the market. Choose one which resembles breast milk as closely as possible. A baby health clinic sister or dietitian will be able to advise you about the best formulae to use.

Soya bean milk substitutes are especially useful for children whose parents who do not wish to use cow's milk. But it's important to remember that not all soya milks on the market are suitable for infants as they may not contain all the nutrients needed for proper growth. Make sure that you choose a *fortified* variety, available from chemists.

Fortified soya milks designed specially for infants (but also suitable for older children and adults) can be recognised in the following ways:

- the container will be labelled "suitable for infants"

- instructions for mixing the feed should be clearly written on the label

- powdered formula should contain a measuring scoop in the can

- liquid formula should give clear instruction for dilution with water

- labels should list the range of vitamins and minerals the formula provides.

Goat's milk is often considered to be a natural food for babies. It has the reputation of being similar to breast milk in composition. This is very far from the truth. In fact, goat's milk bears a greater resemblance to cow's milk and, if used for feeding infants, should never be raw. Goat's milk should always be boiled and diluted with water. The mixture should also be fortified with lactose (the sugar of milk), a multivitamin supplement and extra folic acid (50 micrograms a day). Parents should see a dietitian or a baby health clinic sister for further guidance about the suitability of goat's milk for young children.

Skim milk or low-fat milk should never be used for infants. These milks are deficient in the fat-soluble vitamins like A and D, and are too low in kilojoules. Put simply, low-fat milks cannot provide infants with the necessary nourishment for proper growth and development.

INTRODUCING SOLIDS

Solid foods become important when the infant is about 4 to 5 months old. It is around this time that the demands of growth begin to outstrip the nutriment provided by milk alone. Solid foods will be used to make up the deficiencies of milk and therefore need to be as nutritious as possible.

Vegetarian babies are weaned in the same way as other infants. Good first foods are: baby cereal fortified with iron, e.g. rice cereal; vegetables like potatoes, carrots and pumpkin; and fruit, e.g. bananas, apples and pears. Custards made with milk and cornflour or rice flour are also useful.

It is a good idea to introduce foods one at a time. This gives the child a chance to acquire a taste for a new flavour and also allows the parents to see if a new food provokes a sensitivity. It's not wise to add salt or sugar to the baby's food as these flavours are very addictive. Parents often find that once the children get a taste for salt and sugar they refuse to eat food in its natural state.

A little later

As vegetarian children grow older, soft nutritious foods like cottage cheese, ricotta cheese, yoghurt, eggs and cooked and pureed legumes like dried beans, peas and lentils can all be used. Milk will continue to provide most of the nourishment at this stage and should be offered four or five times a day.

Further on

All children need to experience harder foods they can hold themselves. Hard cheese, bread fingers, toast, chopped fruit or raw vegetables all make excellent finger foods for vegetarian children. At this stage different colours, textures and flavours can be used to stimulate a child's interest in food. It is also at this stage that food from the family pot will start to figure in the child's diet.

All children have times when their diets become very limited and when they will only eat a few favourite foods. These fads are often short-lived and are usually attention-seeking ploys on the part of the child. Faced with a fussy eater, parents should try not to worry — it's often much easier to play along rather than create a fuss. Force-feeding never works and will only aggravate matters.

VEGETARIAN
FOOD FOR
OLDER CHILDREN

Although vegetarian diets can be just as nutritious as other diets, there are some nutrients that require special consideration. Without careful planning the following nutrients are likely to be limited in a child's diet:

- protein

- iron

- calcium

- zinc

- riboflavin

- vitamin B_{12}

These nutrients will be discussed one by one, and we will suggest easy ways to incorporate them into a diet.

Note
The following notes provide guidelines for the amount of each nutrient needed daily by a child. It is wise to aim for these quantities but don't worry if your child's diet does not meet them every day. The recommended amounts are quite generous; most children will come to no harm if their diets occasionally fall short.

PROTEIN FROM LEGUMES (PULSES) + PROTEIN FROM GRAINS = useful protein

BEANS   +   **BREAD**   =   Baked beans on toast
(legume protein)   (grain protein)   (useful protein)
LENTILS   +   **RICE**   =   Lentil curry and rice
(legume protein)   (grain protein)   (useful protein)

PROTEIN FROM SEEDS AND NUTS + PROTEIN FROM GRAINS = useful protein

CASHEWS OR   +   **BREAD**   =   Cashew nut or
PEANUTS   (grain protein)   peanut butter sandwich
(nut protein)   (useful protein)
WALNUTS   +   **PASTA**   =   Spaghetti in walnut sauce
(nut protein)   (grain protein)   (useful protein)
SESAME OR   +   **BREAD**   =   Loaves or rolls with seeds
PUMPKIN SEEDS   (grain protein)   included or sprinkled on
(seed protein)   top
                                                  (useful protein)

DAIRY PROTEIN COMPLEMENTS ANY PLANT PROTEIN

PASTA   +   **CHEESE**   =   Macaroni cheese
(grain protein)   (milk protein)   (useful protein)
RICE   +   **MILK**   =   Sweet rice pudding
(grain protein)   (milk protein)   or savoury creamed rice
                                                  (useful protein)
BREAKFAST   +   **MILK**   =   Porridge or
CEREAL   (milk protein)   cereal with milk
(grain protein)   (useful protein)

PROTEIN

The amount of protein is often used as a hallmark of the goodness of food. Soya beans are said to be nutritious because they are loaded with protein — the same goes for nuts and seeds. But, although true, this is only half the story. We are not only concerned with the amount of protein in a food, we also need to know how good that protein is and how useful it will be to us. When we say "useful" we mean how well the body can put the protein to work. Animal foods, e.g. meat, fish, eggs, milk and cheese, have protein that is very useful. If a child ate only one type of animal protein, say only eggs, she would still grow properly. But a plant food, used as the only source of protein, is not so useful. A child fed high-protein soya beans only, for example, would still lack some nourishment necessary for proper growth.

This problem can be overcome because, if certain plant proteins are mixed together, they will complement each other. That is, any deficiencies in one plant protein can be corrected by the strengths of another. Plant protein combinations can be as useful as any animal protein and will enable children to grow and develop properly.

How do you know which plant proteins to mix together? It has been known for many years that certain plant foods eaten together make very nutritious combinations. Look at the chart opposite and you will probably discover that you have been complementing proteins without realising it!

Milk, dairy products and eggs make protein complements easy. With Vegan diets, however, we need to be more careful. A fortified soya milk (see page 7) is strongly recommended for Vegans. Meals should be planned to include proteins that help each other become useful.

Using the ideas outlined here you can make up your own recipes, such as rice and bean casseroles or lentil patties with cheese, sesame or pumpkin seeds.

Even the small amount of protein in vegetables like potatoes, carrots and broccoli will help to complement the protein in other foods. The main message is to eat a mixture of foods in the same meal.

IRON

Iron is needed for proper formation and function of the blood. Children over 1 year need about 10 mg of iron per day.

Although meat is the richest source of iron, other foods also contain this valuable nutrient. These are:

- beans, peas and lentils (e.g. $\frac{1}{3}$ cup of cooked lentils contains 1 mg iron, $\frac{1}{2}$ cup of cooked lima beans (butter beans) contains 1.5 mg of iron);

- dark green vegetables, especially the leafy kind (e.g. $\frac{1}{3}$ cup of silver beet or spinach contains 1.8 mg iron, $\frac{1}{2}$ cup of cooked broccoli flower pieces contains 0.5 mg of iron);

- breakfast cereals, often containing iron (check labels);

- baby cereals (e.g. 1 level tablespoon of rice cereal contains 3.5 mg of iron);

- soya milks, often fortified with iron (see page 7) (e.g. 1 cup of Prosobee contains 3 mg of iron, 1 cup of Soyagen contains 1.8 mg of iron).

Important note
Iron from plant sources is not easily absorbed by the body. But iron absorption can be improved if some food containing vitamin C is consumed in the same meal. Try to serve fruit juice, fruit salad or raw vegetables at all meals.

CALCIUM
Calcium is needed for good bone growth. Children over 1 year need about 500 mg of calcium per day. Milk and dairy foods like cheese and yoghurt are the best and most useful sources of calcium. For example, 1 cup of cow's milk contains 260 mg of calcium and one 3-cm cube of cheese contains 170 mg of calcium.

Children who do not have milk or dairy products should consume fortified soya milk (see page 7). One cup of Prosobee contains 150 mg of calcium and 1 cup of Soyagen contains 100 mg of calcium. This can be given as a drink or used in cooking.

Some vegetables contain calcium, though much less than milk. These include:

- green vegetables (e.g. $\frac{1}{2}$ cup of broccoli flower pieces contains 55 mg of calcium);

- some nuts (e.g. 30 g of almonds (26 nuts) contain 75 mg of calcium and 30 g of walnuts (15 halves) contain 25 mg of calcium).

Leafy vegetables like spinach or silver beet contain calcium but other ingredients in these vegetables prevent the calcium being readily absorbed by the body.

Important note
Whole nuts should *never* be given to young children, as they are easily inhaled.

ZINC

Children over 1 year need about 10 mg of zinc per day. Animal foods are the richest sources of zinc, but zinc is also found in other foods, such as:

- mature dry beans and lentils (e.g. $\frac{1}{2}$ cup of cooked beans contains 0.9–1.0 mg of zinc);

- dried peas (e.g. $\frac{1}{2}$ cup of black-eye peas contains 1.5 mg of zinc);

- milk (e.g. 1 cup of whole milk contains 0.9 mg of zinc and $\frac{1}{2}$ cup of evaporated milk contains 1.5 mg of zinc);

- dairy foods (e.g. a 3-cm cube of cheddar cheese contains 1.0 mg of zinc);

- nuts (e.g. 2 tablespoons of peanut butter contain 0.5 mg of zinc);

- whole grains (e.g. 1 slice of wholemeal (wholewheat) bread contains 0.5 mg of zinc).

Important note

The absorption of zinc from plant foods is, like iron, very variable. Plant foods containing fibre, such as whole grains, dried beans and peas, and nuts, do not allow zinc to be absorbed easily by the body; the food fibre traps the zinc, making it unavailable. Unlike iron, the absorption of zinc is not enhanced by vitamin C. However, zinc absorption in leavened products, e.g. bread, is improved because of the action of yeast on the fibre.

Milk and dairy foods do not contain fibre, so the absorption of zinc from these foods would probably be greater than from plant foods. Children who are not drinking milk will benefit from fortified soya milk (see page 7). One cup of Infasoy contains 0.9 mg of zinc.

RIBOFLAVIN

Riboflavin is an important B-group vitamin. Children over 1 year need about 0.8 mg of riboflavin per day.

Milk is the main source of riboflavin (1 cup contains 0.39 mg of riboflavin), but this vitamin is not found in useful amounts in other dairy foods. Other foods containing riboflavin are:

- eggs (1 large egg contains 0.15 mg of riboflavin);

- fortified breakfast cereal ($\frac{1}{2}$ cup of cornflakes contains about 0.33 mg of riboflavin);

- leafy green vegetables ($\frac{1}{3}$ cup of cooked spinach or silver beet contains 0.1 mg of riboflavin);

- other green vegetables ($\frac{1}{2}$ cup of cooked broccoli flower pieces or $\frac{1}{2}$ cup of cooked green peas contains 0.1 mg of riboflavin);

- dried beans and lentils ($\frac{1}{2}$ cup of cooked lentils contains 0.06 mg of riboflavin);

- fortified soya milks (see page 7) (1 cup of Prosobee contains 0.15 mg of riboflavin and 1 cup of Soyagen contains 0.18 mg of riboflavin);

- bean sprouts ($\frac{1}{2}$ cup of sprouted soya beans contains 0.08 mg of riboflavin);

- yeast spread ($\frac{1}{2}$ teaspoon of Vegemite or Marmite contains 0.25 mg of riboflavin).

VITAMIN B_{12}

Vitamin B_{12} is needed for growth of cells and tissue. Children over 1 year need about 2 mcg of vitamin B_{12} per day. Vitamin B_{12} is found only in animal foods, and in vegetable foods which have undergone microbial fermentation, e.g. soy sauce, sauerkraut and miso (fermented bean curd). If a diet contains milk, cheese or eggs there is usually no problem. For example:

- eggs (1 large egg contains 1 mcg of B_{12})

- cheese (a 3-cm cube of cheddar contains 0.6 mcg of B_{12})

- milk (1 cup contains 0.7 mcg of B_{12})

- dried milk powder (1 tablespoon of skim milk powder contains 0.4 mcg of B_{12}).

However, strict vegetarians, Vegans, need to ensure that their children get enough vitamin B_{12} from fortified soya milks (see page 7). (One cup of Prosobee contains 0.5 mcg of vitamin B_{12} and one cup of Soyagen contains 1.8 mcg of vitamin B_{12}.) Vitamin supplements containing vitamin B_{12} can also be purchased from local chemists and supermarkets. Check labels for doses.

GUIDELINES
FOR A
BALANCED
DIET

MILK AND MILK PRODUCTS

There is no doubt that these foods are very useful in the diet of vegetarian children. They provide useful protein and can make the preparation of adequate meals so much easier. Fortified soya milks (see page 7) can replace ordinary milk. Children over 1 year should be encouraged to consume 600 mL of milk or fortified soya milk each day. The following list contains milk equivalents that can replace liquid milk in the diet:

- hard cheese, like cheddar (30 g = 200 mL milk)

- yoghurt or buttermilk (100 g = 100 mL milk)

- soft, bland cheeses, like cottage or ricotta, which are easy to mash with other foods (130 g of cottage cheese contain the same amount of calcium as 100 mL of milk)

- milk powder (2 tablespoons of skim milk powder = 250 mL milk).

VEGETABLE PROTEIN

Legumes (dried beans, peas, lentils), nuts and seeds can make significant contributions to vegetarian diets (see page 16 for further details). As well as providing protein, these foods contain iron, zinc and B vitamins. Meat analogues, like soy "meat" and textured vegetable protein (TVP), also fall into this group.

Vegetarian children should have some servings of these foods each day (see chart on page 20 for details). One serving would be:

- 1 cup of cooked legumes (e.g. lentils or beans); or

- 4 tablespoons of nut paste (e.g. peanut butter or tahini paste); or

- 20–30 g of dry textured vegetable protein; or

- 30–40 g of meat analogues (e.g. soya "meat"); or

- 1½ tablespoons of nuts or seeds (can be ground and used in cooking).

A Note on Beans

Beans (the dried varieties, not the long green ones), peas and lentils are collectively called legumes or pulses. They are an extremely nutritious group of foods of which many of us are unaware. Most people have no idea about cooking them and turning them into delightful, tasty and nourishing meals. For vegetarian children they are a godsend. Firstly, legumes are an excellent protein source. Combine them with foods made from grains like bread, noodles or rice and you have a first-rate meal. Don't let anyone knock beans on toast.

Secondly, legumes are easy to mash, puree or blend — a real bonus when it comes to feeding infants and children who might not be able to chew food well. Lastly, these foods are cheap and, in their dried form, store well.

When most people think of beans they are turned off by the thought of all the soaking and boiling that needs to be done. It need not be like that. Tinned beans, like kidney or soya beans, are surely the world's most convenient foods. They are opened and heated up in a trice. If you are worried about any additives like sugar or salt, tip the beans into a sieve or colander and rinse them under the tap. Make up bean or lentil purees in bulk and freeze them as described on page 27.

CAUTION!!!

Many raw legumes contain harmful ingredients that are destroyed at about 100°C. If you intend cooking legumes slowly, in a casserole for example, it is always a good idea to boil them separately for about 15 minutes. Just simmering them is not sufficiently reliable to remove all the toxins.

FRUIT AND VEGETABLES

Apart from providing a range of vitamins (A, C, folic acid) and some minerals, this group is useful in helping the body absorb iron from other plant foods.

Fruit or vegetable servings (especially raw) therefore need to be included in the diets of vegetarian children (see chart on page 20 for details). One serving would be:

- $\frac{1}{2}$ cup of cooked vegetable; or
- $\frac{1}{2}$ cup of stewed fruit; or
- 1 cup of raw vegetable (especially tomato, capsicum); or
- $\frac{1}{2}$ cup of fruit juice; or
- 1 piece fruit (especially citrus fruit).

BREAD, CEREALS AND RICE

This group of foods is extremely useful in complementing other forms of protein. It also provides B vitamins and iron. Each day vegetarian children over 1 year need to eat some servings from this group (see chart on page 20 for details). One serving would be:

- 1 slice of bread; or
- $\frac{1}{2}$–$\frac{3}{4}$ cup of breakfast cereal; or
- $\frac{1}{2}$–$\frac{3}{4}$ cup of cooked rice or other grain; or
- $\frac{1}{2}$–$\frac{3}{4}$ cup of cooked pasta; or
- $\frac{1}{2}$ bread roll; or
- 2 cream crackers; or
- 3 wheat biscuits; or
- 3 level tablespoons of baby cereal.

OTHER FOODS

Eggs: Useful, though not essential, in vegetarian diets for children. The main advantages of using eggs are to ensure that some top quality protein is eaten and to open up new cookery horizons. Omelettes, soufflés and quiches are made with eggs. These tasty foods are quick to prepare and are usually enjoyed by children.

Fats: Butter, margarine and oils. These ingredients are good in that they can increase the energy content of the diet, making it easier for children to consume enough energy foods to meet their needs.

PLANNING CHARTS
FOR VEGETARIAN DIETS

A usual day's diet for a vegetarian child 18 months old could be:

MORNING: Cereal and milk or *fortified* soya milk (see page 7)
             Fruit juice
             Egg (if appropriate)
             Bread and butter or margarine
             Nut paste

MIDDAY: Lentil soup*
             Peanut butter sandwich
             Fruit
             Milk or *fortified* soya milk (see page 7)

EVENING: Nutty rissoles* or home-baked beans*
             Vegetables
             Bread and margarine or butter
             Fruit
             Milk or *fortified* soya milk (see page 7)

Snacks of fresh fruit, vegetables, hard cheese etc. can be eaten during the day.
* See recipe

FOODS	SERVINGS	NUMBER OF SERVINGS PER DAY		
		1–3 years	4–6 years	7–12 years
MILK AND MILK PRODUCTS	600 mL milk, yoghurt or buttermilk	1	1	$1\frac{1}{2}$
VEGETABLE PROTEIN	1 cup cooked legumes 4 tablespoons peanut butter $1\frac{1}{2}$ tablespoons seeds or nuts 30–40 g meat analogue 20–30 g textured vegetable protein	$\frac{1}{2}$	1	$1\frac{1}{2}$
FRUIT AND VEGETABLES	$\frac{1}{2}$ cup cooked vegetables $\frac{1}{2}$ cup stewed fruit 1 cup raw vegetables $\frac{1}{2}$ cup fruit juice 1 piece fruit	2–3	3–4	4–5
BREAD, CEREALS AND RICE	1 slice bread $\frac{1}{2}-\frac{3}{4}$ cup breakfast cereal $\frac{1}{2}-\frac{3}{4}$ cup cooked rice or other grain $\frac{1}{2}-\frac{3}{4}$ cup cooked pasta $\frac{1}{2}$ bread roll 2 cream crackers 3 wheat biscuits 3 tablespoons baby cereal	3	3–4	4–5
FATS	1 tablespoon butter 1 tablespoon margarine 1 tablespoon oil 2 tablespoons cream	1	1	1

Adapted from the chart appearing in "Safe Vegetarian Diets for Children", by I. Vyhmeister, V. Register and M. Sonnenberg.

A SPECIAL NOTE ON VEGAN CHILDREN

Diets that are strictly vegetarian, or Vegan, can pose problems for young children. Such diets tend to be very bulky as they contain large quantities of fruits, vegetables and grains. With Vegan diets, large amounts of food need to be eaten to provide enough nutrients. This feature is an advantage for adults as it can prevent overeating and obesity. However, children tend to have small appetites and a limited capacity for bulky foods. It is difficult for children to eat the quantities of fruits, vegetables and grains that provide adequate nourishment for growth. In lacto- or ovo-vegetarian diets this is not such a problem, as milk and eggs contain concentrated useful protein, and foods like cheese are a rich source of energy (kilojoules).

Strict vegetarians can overcome the problem of the bulky nature of their diet by making liberal use of fortified soya milks (see page 7). As well as providing protein, these useful foods contribute vitamins like B_{12} and riboflavin, and minerals like calcium and zinc. These nutrients are difficult to find in a strictly vegetarian diet.

Extra kilojoules can be added to a diet by making use of fattier foods like peanut butter (the smooth variety for young children) and tahini (sesame seed paste) which can be mixed into dishes before serving. These foods have the advantage of adding extra protein too. At a pinch, extra margarine can be added to meals, but remember that this is mainly fat and does not provide protein, minerals or needed vitamins.

These simple ploys will help to make meals more concentrated in nutrients and will reduce the amounts that children have to eat to satisfy their energy needs.

ANSWERS TO SOME COMMON QUESTIONS

Question: I've heard that the composition of goat's milk is very similar to breast milk. Is this true?

Answer: Goat's milk does not possess any magical qualities. Its composition bears no similarity to that of breast milk. In fact, goat's milk is more like cow's milk in its nutrient content. Goat's milk should never be used to feed infants under 6 months — it has entirely the wrong balance of nutrients. It may be more appropriate for older children but should never be used in its raw or unpasteurised form. Before being consumed, raw goat's milk should be boiled and covered until cool.

Question: Vitamin B_{12} is usually found in animal foods. Can it be obtained from foods of vegetable origin too?

Answer: Only vegetable foods that have undergone microbial fermentation contain vitamin B_{12}. These are foods like sauerkraut (fermented cabbage) and miso (fermented bean curd). However, such foods are unreliable sources of vitamin B_{12}.

Yeast, Spirulina and comfrey are other examples of foods often promoted as suitable vitamin B_{12} sources for vegetarians. They are not.

Yeast and Spirulina have an unpredictable vitamin B_{12} content. And comfrey is not only low in vitamin B_{12} but has been shown to be poisonous in animal experiments.

Instead of relying on doubtful foods for vitamin B_{12} it is safer to include some dairy foods or eggs in the diet. Or ensure that soya bean milk, fortified with vitamin B_{12} (see page 7), is consumed as a drink or used in cooking daily. Failing this, a daily vitamin supplement containing vitamin B_{12} should be taken.

Question: Is it true that commercially grown fruits and vegetables have been sprayed with chemicals and lack any useful nutrients? I've been told that organically grown foods are far more nutritious.

Answer: Most fruits and vegetables are sprayed with pesticides and insecticides. This is why it's important to wash them thoroughly before eating or cooking. However, the nutrient content of commercially grown fruit and vegetables rarely suffers. Organically grown foods, although more expensive, are not nutritionally superior to conventionally grown foods.

Question: Is there any benefit in giving large (mega) doses of vitamins and minerals to my child?

Answer: The daily nutritional needs of children have been well spelt out. Most vitamins are required in very small amounts. Large doses are unnecessary and may even be dangerous. The toxic effects of large doses of vitamins A and D have been known for years. Recent reports suggest that large doses of vitamin B_6, previously thought to be harmless, cause permanent damage to the body nerve endings. We also know that gram amounts of vitamin C can cause kidney stones and may increase our requirement for the vitamin so that if the doses are stopped deficiencies are much more likely.

Our understanding of the body's ability to handle large doses of vitamins is still poor. In children there may be subtle, irreversible changes that are difficult to measure yet have profound effects in later life.

Section two

RECIPES

INTRODUCTION
TO RECIPES

Many parents complain that the food they prepare for their children is dull and boring. Perhaps this is because we tend to fall back on the same old favourites — ingredients that are handy and foods that are easy to cook. One way of providing variety and saving time in preparation is to cook food in bulk and freeze it. For example, cook a large quantity of dried beans (pre-soaked overnight) until they are soft, and blend or pass through a sieve. The mush can be frozen in ice-cube trays. When frozen, turn out the bean cubes and store in a plastic bag in the freezer. If you prepare a variety of mashed food cubes, mealtimes will be a cinch — just grab a couple of cubes (beans, potato, pumpkin), cook them in a saucepan and there you are! An egg poacher is helpful here as it allows you to cook separate cubes in each poaching tray. This helps preserve the individual flavour of the foods. As with all frozen foods, it's important to cook thoroughly.

The recipes in this section provide easy-to-prepare, nutritious and interesting food for vegetarian children. Those recipes beginning on page 31 are suitable for babies, aged 6 months or over, who are established on solids. As baby grows, allow the dishes to have a lumpier consistency to encourage the move from strained foods.

The recipes for older children, beginning on page 39, can be enjoyed by the whole family.

We have not included a separate children's desserts section as most desserts *are* vegetarian! Fresh fruit, in any form, is a wonderful food for children. But the occasional cake or sweet biscuit is a welcome treat. We have therefore included a couple of sweet recipes, under the Breads and Pastries heading, that you and your children will enjoy.

Note

Our recipes have been developed without any added salt. Remember that foods like bread, cheese and even milk contain salt. Any decision to use extra salt is, of course, up to you. But we do suggest that before doing so you give the recipes a fair go. Chances are that your children will not notice any difference, they may even prefer the no-added-salt version.

In a few recipes we have included a little sugar. We feel this small amount (namely, 1 or 2 teaspoons) will not encourage a sweet tooth or obesity. Similarly, we have occasionally used cooking sherry or port. The alcohol in these ingredients is removed on boiling and the residue is harmless to children.

RECIPES FOR
VEGETARIAN
BABIES

MAIN COURSES

CHEESY POTATOES

1 small boiled potato
2 tablespoons cottage cheese or
1 teaspoon grated cheese
Milk

Method
Mash potato. Fold together with the cheese. Add enough milk to make into a creamy puree.

CHEESY NOODLES

2 tablespoons cooked noodles
2 tablespoons cottage cheese or
1 teaspoon grated cheese

Method
Blend or mash ingredients together until smooth.

CHEESY CARROTS

2 tablespoons cooked carrots
2 tablespoons cottage or grated cheese

Method
Blend or mash together.

CHEESY, EGGY POTATO

1 tablespoon hard-boiled egg yolk
2 tablespoons boiled potato
1 tablespoon cottage cheese

Method
Blend together or mash for a lumpier consistency.

CREAMY CORN

$\frac{1}{2}$ corn cob or 2 tablespoons corn kernels
1 tablespoon milk

Method
Steam or boil corn cob until tender. Remove corn from cob.
Blend together 2 tablespoons corn kernels and milk to smooth puree.

CREAMY PEAS

2 tablespoons cooked peas
2 tablespoons warm milk
1 tablespoon cottage or ricotta cheese

Method
Blend ingredients together.

BABY GRAVY

1 cup warm milk
1 tablespoon flour
$\frac{1}{2}$ tablespoon margarine or butter

Method
Melt margarine or butter in saucepan. Add flour and cook on a low heat for half a minute. Off the heat, gradually pour in the milk. Stir over heat until the sauce thickens. Cook for a minute. When cool, pour into ice-cube tray and freeze.
Makes 6 × 1-tablespoon serves

BEANS, POTATO AND GRAVY

2 tablespoons cooked beans or cooked
    lentils
2 tablespoons boiled potato
1 tablespoon baby gravy (defrosted)

Method
Mash together or blend for a smoother consistency.

BEANS, RICE AND GRAVY

*2 tablespoons cooked beans or cooked
      lentils*
2 tablespoons cooked rice
1 tablespoon baby gravy (defrosted)

Method
Blend together.

BEANS, NOODLES AND GRAVY

*2 tablespoons cooked beans or cooked
      lentils*
2 tablespoons cooked noodles
1 tablespoon baby gravy (defrosted)

Method
Blend together.

DESSERTS

TAPIOCA AND BANANA

3 tablespoons cooked tapioca
$\frac{1}{2}$ small banana
1 tablespoon milk

Method
Blend or mash together.

APRICOT RICE PUDDING

$\frac{1}{2}$ teaspoon margarine
2 cups milk
2 tablespoons uncooked short-grain rice
2 fresh or canned apricots
2 tablespoons raisins

Method
Place rice in bottom of greased dish. Add milk, apricot halves and raisins. Bake at 180°C (350°F) for $1\frac{1}{2}$ hours. Blend well.

BAKED EGG CUSTARD

600 mL milk
3 egg yolks
1 banana

Method
Blend together egg yolks, milk and banana and pour into greased dish. Stand in a baking tray half filled with water and bake at 180°C (350°F) for about 20 minutes or until set.

FRUIT AND COTTAGE OR RICOTTA CHEESE

2 tablespoons tinned or fresh fruit, e.g.
peaches, pears or apples
3 tablespoons cottage or ricotta cheese

Method
Blend thoroughly.

HOME-MADE YOGHURT

1 L UHT milk
1 tablespoon natural yoghurt
Clean glass jars or empty yoghurt
containers

Method
1. Heat milk to the point where you can *just* bear to keep your finger in it for no more than a count to 10.
2. Beat the yoghurt with some of the milk to make a runny mixture.
3. Add milk/yoghurt mixture to rest of milk.
4. Warm the glass jars or the empty yoghurt containers with hot water.
5. Fill containers with yoghurt, put into a large bowl and insulate with a blanket or a couple of towels.
6. Allow to set in a warm place overnight, store in fridge.

FRUIT AND YOGHURT

As for Fruit and Cottage or Ricotta Cheese, but use yoghurt instead of cottage cheese.

RECIPES
FOR VEGETARIAN
CHILDREN

DIPS, SPREADS AND FILLINGS

Serve the following dips with a range of fresh vegetable "dippers", e.g. celery sticks, cucumber sticks, carrot sticks. Also use steamed French beans and pieces of pita bread cut into strips and dried in the oven.

EGGPLANT (AUBERGINE) DIP

2 medium eggplants
1 crushed clove garlic (optional)
3 tablespoons yoghurt
Juice of $\frac{1}{2}$ lemon (approx.)
Chopped parsley or fresh coriander

Method
1. Prick eggplants with fork.
2. Bake on baking tray in oven at 180°C (350°F) until soft, or grill, turning frequently. Leave to cool.
3. Take skins off and mash flesh to a pulp or blend in liquidiser.
4. Add garlic, yoghurt, lemon juice and herbs to taste.

GUACAMOLE

2 medium ripe avocados
2 medium skinned tomatoes
(or use canned)
1 small onion, chopped
2 teaspoons yoghurt
Juice of $\frac{1}{2}$ lemon (approx.)

Method
1. Peel avocados and blend in liquidiser with tomatoes and onion.
2. Add yoghurt and lemon juice to taste.

RICOTTA CREAM WITH CHIVES

150 mL milk
150 g ricotta cheese
Chopped chives or spring onion tops

Method
1. Heat milk to boiling point.
2. Blend milk and ricotta cheese in blender till smooth.
3. Pour into serving container and allow to cool.
4. Stir in chopped chives or onion tops.

PEANUT BUTTER

250 g peanuts without shells
Vegetable oil

Method
1. Roast peanuts in oven at 180°C (350°F) until skins will easily rub off (or use unsalted pre-roasted peanuts).
2. Grind in a liquidiser or grinder.
3. Put ground nut meal into a bowl.
4. Add enough oil to make a spreadable paste.
5. Store in fridge.

TOFU

250 g soya flour
600 mL water
Juice of 2 lemons
Chopped mixed herbs (optional)

Method
1. In a bowl mix some of the water with the soya flour to form lump-free paste.
2. Add rest of water.
3. Bring to boil in a saucepan.
4. Add lemon juice and cool (the mixture will thicken dramatically).
5. Strain through a cheesecloth or a clean pair of tights stretched over a colander, and leave to drain overnight.
6. Mix in chopped herbs.
Use as filling in sandwiches.

SOUPS

SPLIT PEA AND MACARONI SOUP

$\frac{1}{2}$ cup dry split peas

4 cups water

1 medium onion

1 celery stick

1 medium carrot

2 tablespoons polyunsaturated
    margarine

2 teaspoons Worcestershire sauce

Pepper

Pinch mixed herbs

$\frac{1}{2}$ cup dry macaroni

1 teaspoon finely chopped parsley

Method

1. Place split peas in a bowl and cover with the water. Soak for 1 hour.

2. Place split peas in a saucepan with water. Add more water to make about 1 litre if necessary.

3. Bring to the boil and simmer gently for 15 minutes.

4. Finely chop onion, celery and carrot. Sauté in margarine until golden brown.

5. Add to lentils with Worcestershire sauce, pepper and herbs, and continue to cook for 15 minutes.

6. Add macaroni and cook for a further 15–20 minutes, or until macaroni is cooked and vegetables are tender.

7. Stir in parsley and serve.

Serves 6–8

FRESH SPINACH SOUP

1 small onion, finely chopped
1 small potato, washed and cubed
1 tablespoon oil
4 cups water
4 heaped tablespoons skim milk powder
12 spinach leaves, without stalks
½ teaspoon grated nutmeg

Method

1. Fry onions and potato in oil for 3 minutes.

2. Add 3 cups water and simmer till potato is cooked.

3. In a blender combine 1 cup water and skim milk powder, then add to potato and onion mixture.

4. Wash spinach leaves and heat without water until just cooked — spinach should not lose colour.

5. Blend spinach with half the potato/milk mixture.

6. Reheat with rest of potato/milk mixture and stir in nutmeg. Serve hot.

Serves 4

MINTED CARROT SOUP

5 carrots
1 medium onion
1 large potato
2 shallots
3 tablespoons polyunsaturated
 margarine
1 clove garlic, crushed
4 cups water
2 teaspoons sugar
Pepper
2 tablespoons finely chopped parsley
2 teaspoons finely chopped mint
½ cup cream

Method

1. Peel and slice carrots, onion and potato. Chop shallots.

2. Melt margarine and cook carrots, onion, shallots, potato and garlic for 5 minutes. Do not allow to colour.

3. Add water, sugar and pepper. Simmer gently for 1 hour.

4. Stir in parsley and mint.

5. Blend mixture until smooth, then return to saucepan.

6. Stir in cream and reheat gently over a low heat, without boiling.

Serves 6–8

SWEET CORN SOUP

1 tablespoon polyunsaturated
*   margarine*
1 small onion
3 celery sticks
2 shallots
2 potatoes
1 × 440 g can corn kernels
600 mL water
Pepper
Finely chopped parsley

Method

1. Finely chop onion, celery, shallots and potatoes and sauté in melted margarine.
2. Add corn kernels, water and pepper.
3. Bring to the boil and simmer gently for 30 minutes or until vegetables are tender.
4. Serve garnished with finely chopped parsley.
Serves 6–8

OLD-FASHIONED VEGETABLE SOUP

$\frac{1}{4}$ cup dry red beans
$\frac{1}{4}$ cup split peas
$\frac{1}{4}$ cup dry lentils
$\frac{1}{4}$ cup barley
4 carrots
1 medium onion
$\frac{1}{3}$ cup chopped turnip
1 potato
2 celery sticks
2 tablespoons polyunsaturated
*   margarine*
5 cups water
$1\frac{1}{2}$ teaspoons tomato paste
Pepper
$\frac{1}{2}$ teaspoon mixed herbs

Method

1. Place red beans, split peas, lentils and barley in a basin and cover with water. Soak for at least 1 hour.
2. Peel and finely chop carrots, onion, turnip and potato. Chop celery.
3. Sauté in melted margarine for 5 minutes.
4. Add water, tomato paste, pepper and herbs.
5. Drain pre-soaked beans and vegetables and add to saucepan.
6. Bring to the boil and simmer for 1 hour or until all ingredients are tender.
Serves 6–8

LENTIL SOUP

*1 tablespoon polyunsaturated
    margarine*
1 medium onion
1 medium carrot
1 celery stick
1 pinch thyme
Pepper
750 mL hot water
$\frac{1}{3}$ cup dry lentils, washed
1 tablespoon finely chopped parsley
1 × 425 g can peeled tomatoes
Grated cheese

Method

1. Finely chop onion, carrot and celery and sauté in margarine for 1 minute.
2. Add thyme and pepper.
3. Add water, lentils, parsley and tomatoes to onion mixture.
4. Simmer gently for 45 minutes.
5. Place a small amount of grated cheese in bowls and pour in soup.
For a smoother, thicker soup, blend mixture before serving.
Serves 6–8

COLD CUCUMBER AND YOGHURT SOUP

500 g peeled cucumber
1 teaspoon white sugar
650 mL natural yoghurt
1 tablespoon chopped fresh mint
1 cup milk (approx.)

Method

1. Blend cucumber, sugar and 600 mL yoghurt until smooth.
2. Add chopped mint.
3. Stir in milk until desired consistency is achieved.
4. Cool in fridge until well chilled.
5. Serve with 1 tablespoon yoghurt stirred into each serve.
Serves 4

ENTREES

ASPARAGUS BREADCASES

10–12 slices bread
Polyunsaturated margarine (for spreading)
1 tablespoon flour
1 tablespoon polyunsaturated margarine
150 mL milk
Pepper
1 cup cooked asparagus

Method

1. Trim crusts off bread and spread one side of bread with margarine.

2. Place bread with margarine side down in patty cake tin.

3. Bake at 190°F (375°F) for 10–15 minutes, or until golden brown and crisp.

4. Melt margarine in a saucepan. Stir in flour and cook over a low heat for 1 minute.

5. Gradually stir in milk and thicken over a low heat, stirring continuously. Season with pepper.

6. Stir in mashed asparagus.

7. Spoon mixture into breadcases and return to oven for 10–15 minutes, or until heated through.

Makes 10–12

SWEET CORN BREADCASES

10–12 slices bread
Polyunsaturated margarine (for
    spreading)
1 tablespoon flour
1 tablespoon polyunsaturated
    margarine
150 mL milk
Pepper
1 cup corn kernels

Method
1. Trim crusts off bread and spread one side of bread with margarine.
2. Place bread with margarine side down in patty cake tin.
3. Bake at 190°C (375°F) for 10–15 minutes or until golden brown and crisp.
4. Melt 1 tablespoon margarine in a saucepan. Stir in flour and cook over a low heat for 1 minute.
5. Gradually stir in milk and thicken over a low heat, stirring continuously. Season with pepper.
6. Stir in corn kernels.
7. Spoon mixture into breadcases and return to oven for 10–15 minutes, or until heated through.
Makes 10–12

CHEESE AND ONION BREADCASES

10–12 slices bread
Polyunsaturated margarine (for
    spreading)
1 tablespoon flour
1 tablespoon polyunsaturated
    margarine
150 mL milk
2 tablespoons finely chopped onion
2 tablespoons finely chopped red
    capsicum
1 teaspoon finely chopped parsley
1 cup grated tasty cheese
Pepper

Method
1. Trim crusts off bread and spread one side of bread with margarine.
2. Place bread with margarine side down in patty cake tin.
3. Bake at 190°C (375°F) for 10–15 minutes or until golden brown and crisp.
4. Melt 1 tablespoon margarine in a saucepan. Stir in flour and cook over a low heat for 1 minute.
5. Gradually stir in milk and thicken over a low heat, stirring continuously. Season with pepper.
6. Stir in onion, capsicum, parsley and cheese.

7. Spoon mixture into bread cases and return to oven for 10–15 minutes, or until heated through.
Makes 10–12

INDIVIDUAL VEGETABLE QUICHES

Pastry

$\frac{1}{4}$ cup white flour

$\frac{3}{4}$ cup wholemeal (wholewheat) flour

2 tablespoons polyunsaturated
  margarine

1 egg

Iced water

Filling

1 small onion

1 stick celery

1 small carrot

$\frac{1}{4}$ capsicum

1 tablespoon oil

$\frac{3}{4}$ cup grated cheese

2 eggs

100 mL milk

100 mL cream

Pinch nutmeg

Pepper

Method

1. Sift flours into a bowl and rub in margarine, using fingertips, until mixture resembles breadcrumbs.

2. Make a well in the centre of the flour mixture and add egg with a small amount of iced water and mix well, adding just enough water to form a firm dough.

3. Wrap in plastic and refrigerate for 20 minutes.

4. Roll out pastry and line individual quiche dishes.

5. Refrigerate for a further 10 minutes.

6. Bake blind at 190°C (375°F) for 15–20 minutes.

7. Finely chop vegetables for filling and fry lightly in oil.

8. Beat cheese with eggs, milk, cream, nutmeg and pepper.

9. Pour mixture into each prepared quiche dish.

10. Sprinkle vegetable mixture over each dish evenly.

11. Bake at 190°C (375°F) for 20–30 minutes, or until golden brown and set.

To blind bake: place a piece of greaseproof paper over pastry in tin and pour in rice, dried beans or the like to keep pastry from rising.
Makes 6

STUFFED MUSHROOMS

6 large mushrooms
1 teaspoon polyunsaturated margarine,
*   melted*
1 tablespoon polyunsaturated oil
1 tablespoon finely chopped onion
1 tablespoon finely chopped red
*   capsicum*
1 tablespoon cream cheese
1 tablespoon milk
Pinch paprika
2 tablespoons grated tasty cheese
1 teaspoon polyunsaturated margarine
1 tablespoon breadcrumbs
1 teaspoon finely chopped parsley

Method

1. Trim stalks of mushrooms level with caps. Finely chop stalks and reserve for filling.
2. Wipe mushrooms with a damp cloth, brush rounded side with melted margarine and place on a baking tray.
3. Heat oil and fry chopped onion, capsicum and mushroom stalks for 5 minutes.
4. Remove from heat and drain off oil. Allow to cool.
5. Beat together cream cheese and milk until smooth; add paprika.
6. Fold in onion mixture and mix well.
7. Spoon mixture into mushrooms and sprinkle with cheese.
8. Melt margarine in a small saucepan and remove from heat. Stir in breadcrumbs and sprinkle over mushrooms.
9. Bake at 190°C (375°F) for 15 minutes or until tender and golden brown.
10. Garnish with finely chopped parsley.
Serves 3

CREAMED POTATOES

2 large potatoes
1 celery stick
$\frac{1}{2}$ red capsicum
1 medium onion
1 shallot
1 tablespoon polyunsaturated
*   margarine*
$\frac{1}{2}$ cup sour cream
50 mL milk
1 teaspoon finely chopped parsley
1 teaspoon sesame seeds
Pepper
1 hard-boiled egg
Pinch paprika
1 tablespoon breadcrumbs

Method

1. Peel and dice potatoes, and cook in boiling water until just tender (about 10 minutes).

2. Slice celery diagonally, dice red capsicum, onion and shallot, and sauté in margarine until just tender (about 5 minutes).
3. Lightly fold through potato and keep warm.
4. Mix together sour cream, milk, parsley, sesame seeds and pepper. Fold through potato mixture.
5. Spoon into serving dish and sprinkle with roughly chopped boiled egg, paprika and breadcrumbs.
6. Brown under grill and serve.
Serves 4

PIZZA

Base

1 packet dry yeast
$\frac{1}{4}$ cup milk
1 egg
$1\frac{1}{2}$ cups flour
$\frac{1}{2}$ teaspoon sugar
3 teaspoons polyunsaturated margarine

Sauce

2 tablespoons tomato paste
1 medium tomato
1 clove garlic

Topping

2 medium tomatoes
$\frac{1}{2}$ capsicum
1 small onion
6 mushrooms
2 pineapple rings
1 cup grated mozzarella cheese
1 cup grated tasty cheese

Method

1. Warm milk and add crumbled yeast. Stir until dissolved and add beaten egg.
2. Sift flour and sugar together.
3. Rub in margarine, using fingertips, until mixture resembles breadcrumbs.
4. Make a well in the centre of the flour mixture and pour in yeast mixture. Mix well.
5. Leave to stand in a warm place until pastry doubles in volume.
6. Roll out pastry until about 1 cm thick and large enough to cover pizza tray.
7. Lightly oil pizza tray and cover with pastry.
8. Peel tomato for sauce and blend with remaining sauce ingredients until smooth.
9. Spoon sauce over pastry evenly and top with sliced tomatoes, capsicum, onion, mushrooms and chopped pineapple.
10. Sprinkle grated cheeses on top.
11. Bake at 220°C (425°F) for about 20 minutes, or until pastry is golden brown and crisp.
Serves 4–5

PANCAKES

$\frac{1}{4}$ cup white flour
$\frac{1}{4}$ cup wholemeal (wholewheat) flour
1 egg
$\frac{1}{2}$ cup milk

Method

1. Sift dry ingredients into a bowl.
2. Beat in eggs, one at a time.
3. Gradually stir in milk until batter is smooth.
4. Let stand for 30 minutes.
5. Heat a lightly greased pancake pan over a gentle heat.
6. Pour about 2–3 tablespoons of mixture into pan and swirl around evenly. Cook until light golden brown on that side, then turn and cook other side.
7. Repeat with remaining batter.
8. Place filling on half of the pancake and roll up securely. Serve garnished with parsley.

Makes 4–6

ASPARAGUS AND MUSHROOM PANCAKES

1 quantity pancakes (see recipe)
3 large mushrooms
1 shallot
1 tablespoon polyunsaturated
    margarine
Pepper
1 × 440 g tin asparagus

Sauce

$1\frac{1}{2}$ tablespoons polyunsaturated
    margarine
$1\frac{1}{2}$ tablespoons flour
200 mL milk
$\frac{1}{2}$ cup grated tasty cheese

Method

1. Dice shallot and slice mushrooms.
2. Melt margarine and sauté until soft. Add pepper.
3. Add asparagus and let warm through on a very low heat.
4. Place spoonfuls onto half of pancake and roll up securely and place in a baking dish. Keep warm while making sauce.
5. Melt margarine in a saucepan. Add flour and cook over heat for 1 minute.
6. Gradually stir in milk and thicken over heat.
7. Add $\frac{1}{3}$ cup cheese and stir through till melted.

8. Spoon sauce over pancakes and sprinkle remaining grated cheese on top.
9. Place in oven at 180°C (350°F) for 5–10 minutes till heated through. Brown under grill.
Makes 4–6

RICOTTA AND SPINACH PANCAKES

1 quantity pancakes (see recipe)
5 spinach leaves
$\frac{1}{2}$ cup ricotta cheese
Pinch nutmeg
Pepper

Sauce

3 tablespoons polyunsaturated
*   margarine*
3 tablespoons flour
Pinch nutmeg
Pepper
$1\frac{1}{4}$ cups milk
1 cup grated cheddar cheese

Method
1. Wash spinach, place in boiling water and half cook (about 5 minutes).
2. Cream ricotta cheese in a bowl.
3. Drain spinach and chop finely. Add to ricotta cheese with nutmeg and pepper. Mix well.

4. Place spoonful of mixture on half of each pancake, roll up securely and place in a baking dish. Keep warm while making sauce.
5. Melt margarine in a saucepan. Mix nutmeg and pepper with flour, stir into margarine and cook over a low heat for 1 minute.
6. Gradually stir in milk and thicken over a low heat, stirring continuously.
7. Stir in grated cheese until sauce is smooth.
8. Pour sauce over pancakes and garnish with parsley.
Makes 4–6

VEG TACOS

8 taco shells
2 onions, chopped
1 teaspoon oil
1 tablespoon sweet paprika
500g tinned or fresh tomatoes
500g pumpkin, chopped into small
    pieces
300g tinned sweet corn kernels
1 teaspoon oregano
400g cooked kidney beans (canned are
    fine)
Grated cheese

Method
1. Cook onions in oil until soft but not coloured (about 5 minutes).
2. Add paprika to onions and cook for 1 minute longer.
3 Add tomatoes and juice, pumpkin pieces and liquid from canned sweet corn to onions. Cook uncovered, stirring occasionally, until pumpkin has disintegrated and mixture is thick.
4. Add oregano, beans and sweet corn and cook for further 5 minutes. Mixture should be thick.
5. Meanwhile, heat taco shells under grill or in oven.
6. Fill taco shells with pumpkin mixture and sprinkle with grated cheese.
7. Serve with green salad.
Serves 8

NUTTY RISSOLES

1 small onion
1 stick celery
$\frac{1}{2}$ red capsicum
1 small carrot
3 mushrooms
3 teaspoons polyunsaturated margarine
$\frac{1}{3}$ cup finely ground nuts
1 egg
2 tablespoons tomato sauce
1 teaspoon chopped parsley
1 teaspoon lemon juice
$\frac{1}{3}$ cup grated cheese
$\frac{1}{4}$ teaspoon Worcestershire sauce
$\frac{1}{4}$ cup soft breadcrumbs
$\frac{1}{4}$ cup flour
Pinch herbs
Pepper
Breadcrumbs for coating

Method
1. Dice onion, celery, capsicum, carrot and mushrooms.
2. Fry in margarine until golden brown.
3. Combine with nuts, egg, tomato sauce, parsley, lemon juice, cheese, Worcestershire sauce, breadcrumbs, flour, herbs and pepper.
4. Roll into 4 rissoles and coat in breadcrumbs.
5. Refrigerate for 30 minutes.
6. Fry until golden brown and serve.
Makes 4

MAIN COURSES

EGG PUFFS

1 shallot
1 tomato
2 teaspoons polyunsaturated margarine
$\frac{1}{4}$ teaspoon chopped parsley
$2\frac{1}{2}$ tablespoons cream
$2\frac{1}{2}$ tablespoons milk
4 eggs
$\frac{1}{3}$ cup grated cheese
Pepper
1 packet ready-made puff pastry

Method
1. Chop shallot and tomato and sauté in margarine with parsley.
2. Beat cream with the milk, eggs, cheese and pepper.
3. Pour in with tomato and shallot and cook lightly until mixture appears like scrambled eggs.
4. Roll out pastry into an oblong 30 × 15 cm and cut into 4 equal pieces.
5. Spoon egg mixture, towards one side, equally between pastry sheets.
6. Fold over, sealing edges by glazing with milk or water.
7. Glaze outside with milk or water and bake at 220°C (425°F) for 20–25 minutes, or until golden brown.
Makes 4

STUFFED ZUCCHINI (COURGETTES)

2 large zucchini
1 small onion
2 mushrooms
1 medium tomato
1 teaspoon polyunsaturated margarine
1 clove garlic
Pinch oregano
Pepper
2 tablespoons brown rice
1 cup water
2 eggs
$\frac{1}{2}$ cup grated cheese

Method

1. Slice zucchini in half lengthwise and carefully scoop out pulp.
2. Dice onion and mushrooms.
3. Peel and dice tomato and sauté in margarine with onions, mushrooms, crushed garlic, oregano and pepper.
4. Add rice and water. Cover and let simmer until rice is tender, about 15–20 minutes. Water should have evaporated.
5. Beat in eggs.
6. Spoon mixture into zucchini shells, being careful not to overfill as this could cause the shells to split.
7. Place in a baking dish with a small amount of water, cover with foil and bake at 190°C (375°F) until shells are tender, about 20 minutes.
8. Sprinkle with grated cheese and grill until golden brown.
Serves 4

MILD VEGETABLE CURRY

1 medium onion, sliced
1 tablespoon oil
Small piece fresh ginger, chopped
1 teaspoon curry powder
2 large potatoes, cubed
3 medium carrots, sliced
$\frac{1}{2}$ capsicum, sliced
150 g green beans, sliced
150 mL canned coconut milk
150 mL water

Method

1. Fry onion till soft.
2. Add ginger and fry for 30 seconds.
3. Add curry powder and cook for 20 seconds.
4. Add vegetables, coconut milk and water.
5. Simmer with lid on for 15 minutes.
6. Cook with lid off till vegetables are soft. Serve with dhal and yoghurt.
Serves 4–6

MURPHY BAKE

*Potatoes baked in their jackets and
    served with a variety of sauces.*

1 large potato per person

Method
1. Scrub each potato thoroughly and prick all over with fork.
2. Bake in oven for about 45 minutes at 200°C (400°F) until easily pierced with sharp knife.

PEANUT SAUCE

$\frac{1}{2}$ *cup crunchy peanut butter*

1 small onion

1 teaspoon honey

2 tablespoons lemon juice

2 teaspoons soy sauce

1 cup milk (approx.)

Method
1. Boil milk.
2. Blend other ingredients thoroughly.
3. Add hot milk to blender to achieve a runny consistency.
4. Pour into serving dish (sauce thickens on standing).

RICOTTA AND CHIVE SAUCE

150g ricotta cheese

150 mL milk

Chopped chives or onion tops

Method
1. Heat milk to boiling point.
2. Blend hot milk and cheese thoroughly.
3. Pour into serving container and allow to cool.
4. Stir in chives or spring onion tops.

BEAN SAUCE

$\frac{1}{2}$ *cup cooked kidney beans (canned are
    fine)*

1 small chopped onion

1 tablespoon chutney or pickle

$\frac{1}{2}$ *cup milk*

Method
1. Bring milk to boil.
2. Blend other ingredients till smooth.
3. Add hot milk to ingredients in blender to achieve runny consistency.
4. Pour into serving container.
5. Serve with a bowl of grated cheddar cheese.

NUT LOAF

Pastry

1 cup wholemeal (wholewheat) flour

1 cup white flour

½ cup margarine

1 egg yolk (save egg white for glazing)

1 tablespoon lemon juice

2 tablespoons iced water

Filling

2 large mushrooms

½ cup chopped celery

½ cup chopped onion

1 tablespoon oil

Pepper

Pinch herbs

1 medium piece pumpkin

¼ cup chopped almonds

½ cup chopped walnuts

½ cup chopped cashews

¼ cup grated carrot

1 tablespoon chopped parsley

¼ cup oats

2 teaspoons sesame seeds

½ cup cottage cheese

1 egg

1 tablespoon tomato sauce

½ teaspoon Worcestershire sauce

Method

1. Sift dry ingredients together.

2. Rub in margarine with fingertips until the mixture resembles fine breadcrumbs.

3. Add egg yolk, lemon juice and water and mix to a firm dough.

4. Save quarter of dough. Roll out remaining dough, to line base and sides of loaf tin. Line tin and bake blind* for 10–15 minutes at 190°C (375°F).

5. Chop mushrooms, celery and onion.

6. Sauté in 1 tablespoon oil. Add pepper and herbs.

7. Cook pumpkin and mash.

8. Chop up all nuts finely.

9. Combine all ingredients together and mix through.

10. Place mixture into prepared pastry tin and roll out remaining quarter of pastry to form top.

11. Glaze edges with egg white, place pastry on top and pinch edges together. Glaze and place in oven at 190°C (375°F) for 60–75 minutes.

12. Allow to cool in tin for 10 minutes before turning out. May be served hot or cold.

*To blind bake: place a piece of greaseproof paper over pastry in tin and pour in rice, dried beans or the like to keep pastry from rising.

Serves 4–6

DHAL

1 small onion
1 tablespoon oil
1 teaspoon coriander seeds
1 teaspoon cumin seeds
½ teaspoon whole cloves
1 cm cinnamon stick
1 cup red lentils
150 mL canned coconut milk
150 mL water
1 teaspoon black mustard seeds
Fresh coriander leaves, chopped

Method
1. Fry onion in ½ tablespoon of oil till soft.
2. Grind coriander seeds, cumin seeds, cloves and cinnamon together.
3. Add spices to onion and cook gently for 30 seconds.
4. Add lentils, coconut milk and water and cook covered till lentils are soft (add more water if mixture is dry).
5. Set dhal aside.
6. In clean saucepan fry mustard seeds in rest of oil.
7. When they have stopped popping add dhal and cook mixture for 5 minutes.
8. Add chopped coriander leaves.
Serve with vegetable curry and yoghurt.
Serves 4

HOME-BAKED BEANS

240 g dried white beans
1 large onion, chopped
1 tablespoon oil
2 celery stalks, chopped
2 medium carrots, peeled and chopped
750–800 g tinned tomatoes
2 teaspoons sugar
½ cup red wine or dry sherry
1 cup grated tasty cheese

Method
1. Soak beans until they are swollen, then boil in water until almost cooked, drain and set aside.
2. Fry onion in oil until soft.
3. Add celery and carrot and continue frying for 1 minute.
4. Add tomatoes, sugar, wine or sherry.
5. Simmer uncovered until the tomatoes disintegrate.
6. Pour into an oven dish and add beans.
7. Cook in oven at 200°C (400°F) for 1 hour.
8. Sprinkle with grated cheese and return to oven till cheese melts.
Serve with jacket potatoes.
Serves 4

VEGETABLE STEW WITH HEALTHY DUMPLINGS

2 small chopped onions
1 teaspoon oil or butter
500 g sliced zucchini (courgettes)
450 g tomatoes, fresh or tinned

Dumplings

1 L milk
1 tablespoon vinegar or lemon juice
2 eggs
100 g grated cheddar cheese
150 g fresh breadcrumbs

Method

1. Heat milk to boiling point and add vinegar or lemon juice.
2. Stir the milk off the heat until it separates into curds and whey.
3. Carefully pour off whey and reserve.
4. Mash curds with a fork.
5. Beat eggs and add to curds, mixing well.
6. Add breadcrumbs and grated cheese to the egg/curd mixture and mix well.
7. Form into 10 round dumplings and set aside.
8. Boil whey until 600 mL remains.
9. Cook onions in oil until soft but not coloured (about 5 minutes).
10. Add zucchini and tomato and simmer uncovered until zucchini are soft.

11. Put this mixture into ovenproof dish. Arrange the dumplings on top to form one layer. Pour whey over dumplings.
12. Bake in oven at 180°C (350°F) for 30 minutes or until dumplings are brown and crisp.
Serves 4

RED CABBAGE WITH APPLE

1 medium onion, chopped
1 tablespoon oil
500 g shredded red cabbage
2 large apples, peeled and cored
1 tablespoon vinegar
2 teaspoons brown sugar
$\frac{1}{2}$ teaspoon whole cloves
$\frac{1}{3}$ cup water

Method

1. Fry onion in oil till soft.
2. Add cabbage and apple and stir for 30 seconds.
3. Add vinegar, sugar, cloves and water.
4. Cover and simmer for 20 minutes, add more water if mixture becomes dry.
Serve with jacket potatoes and yoghurt.
Serves 4

VEGETABLES AND ALMONDS CHINESE-STYLE

5 cups of sliced vegetables
    (e.g. celery, onion, capsicum, carrot,
    beans, broccoli)
1 cup blanched chopped almonds
1 tablespoon oil
1 tablespoon grated fresh ginger
2 cloves crushed garlic (optional)
1 level tablespoon cornflour
$\frac{1}{4}$ cup cooking sherry or port
1 tablespoon soy sauce
1 teaspoon sugar

Method
1. Fry almonds in $\frac{1}{2}$ the oil, stir until golden, then remove and set aside.
2. Fry ginger (and garlic if used) for 30 seconds.
3. Add the rest of the oil, heat and fry vegetables in hot oil, stirring, for 2 minutes.
4. Put lid on pan and turn heat to low.
5. Cook for further 3 minutes.
6. Mix cornflour with sherry, soy sauce and sugar and add to vegetable mixture.
7. Stir for 1 minute, add water if mixture gets too dry.
8. Stir in almonds.
Serve with boiled rice.
Serves 4

CRISPY-TOPPED FENNEL

4 medium fennel bulbs
1 medium onion, chopped
1 tablespoon oil
350 g peeled tomatoes
$\frac{1}{2}$ cup fresh breadcrumbs
$\frac{1}{2}$ cup strong cheese
Grated rind of half a lemon

Method
1. Slice fennel bulbs into sections about 5 mm thick.
2. Fry onion in oil till soft.
3. Add the fennel and fry, stirring continuously, for about a minute.
4. Add tomatoes and crush till the juice runs, then lower heat to simmering point and simmer till fennel stalk can be pierced by a knife point (add more water if mixture becomes dry).
5. Transfer to an oven dish and sprinkle with the breadcrumbs, cheese and lemon rind.
6. Bake in the oven at 200°C (400°F) till topping is brown and crisp.
Serves 4

WHEAT
AND CELERY BAKE

2 cups chopped celery

1 small onion, chopped

2 tablespoons oil

$\frac{1}{2}$ teaspoon celery seeds

1 cup bulgar (cracked wheat)

$1\frac{1}{2}$ cups milk

$1\frac{1}{2}$ cups water

1 cup grated cheese

1 cup breadcrumbs

Method

1. Sauté celery and onion in oil.

2. Add celery seeds and bulgar and fry gently for 1 minute.

3. Add milk and water and simmer for 15 minutes.

4. Add $\frac{3}{4}$ cheese and turn into casserole dish.

5. Bake in oven at 190°C (375°F) for 10–15 minutes.

6. Sprinkle on cheese and breadcrumbs and cook for further 10 minutes.

Serves 4

RICE AND PASTA DISHES

SAVOURY RICE

1 cup cooked brown rice
2 tablespoons polyunsaturated
   margarine
1 medium onion, chopped
1 shallot, chopped
1 cup sliced mushrooms
1 celery stick, chopped
$\frac{1}{4}$ cup chopped red capsicum
$\frac{1}{2}$ cup corn kernels
$\frac{1}{2}$ cup peas
2 cabbage leaves, shredded
2 hard-boiled eggs
Pepper
$\frac{1}{2}$ cup sour cream or yoghurt

Method

1. Keep cooked rice warm in a colander over a saucepan of boiling water.

2. Melt margarine in a saucepan and add onion, shallot, mushrooms, celery and capsicum. Cook for 5 minutes.

3. Add corn kernels and peas, and cook for a further 5 minutes.

4. Remove from heat and stir in shredded cabbage.

5. Fold mixture through hot rice. Keep warm.

6. Roughly chop eggs and place in a saucepan with pepper and sour cream or yoghurt. Heat through gently. Do not allow to boil as the mixture will curdle.

7. Pour over rice and serve while hot.
Serves 4

CAULIFLOWER ON RICE

1 cup uncooked brown rice
1 small cauliflower

Sauce

2 tablespoons polyunsaturated
*   margarine*
3 tablespoons flour
$\frac{1}{2}$ teaspoon dry mustard
2 cups milk
1 cup grated cheese

Method

1. Boil rice till cooked.
2. Melt margarine and stir in flour.
3. Add mustard.
4. Gradually pour on milk and stir till smooth.
5. Slowly bring to boil, stirring till mixture thickens, and simmer for 10 minutes.
6. Add $\frac{3}{4}$ of the cheese to sauce and stir till smooth.
7. Trim cauliflower and steam until just soft.
8. Put rice on bottom of casserole dish.
9. Place cauliflower on top.
10. Cover with sauce and top with rest of cheese.
11. Cook in oven at 200°C (400°F) for 15 minutes.
Serves 4

SAVOURY-TOPPED PUMPKIN

8 slices butternut pumpkin, cut from end
*   without pips*
1 onion, chopped
1 teaspoon oil
2 cups cooked rice
2 cups grated cheddar cheese
Any of the following, chopped and mixed
*   together:*
Olives
Herbs
Mushrooms
Tomatoes

Method

1. Bake pumpkin slices on greased baking tray at 200°C (400°F) until soft.
2. Meanwhile, cook onion in oil until soft but not coloured (about 5 minutes).
3. When onion is soft add cooked rice and other ingredients but reserve 1 cup of grated cheese.
4. Pile mixture onto pumpkin slices and sprinkle with remaining cheese.
5. Bake in oven for further 10 minutes.
Serves 4–6

PUMPERS À LA MELANIE

4 cups pumpkin chopped into 2-cm
cubes (no need to peel)
1 onion, chopped
1 teaspoon oil
500 g fresh or tinned tomatoes
1 tablespoon cooking sherry or port
1 teaspoon oregano

Method
1. Cook onion in oil until soft but not coloured (about 5 minutes).
2. Add tomatoes, sherry and pumpkin cubes and simmer uncovered, stirring occasionally.
3. When pumpkin is softening add oregano.
4. Cook until pumpkin is very soft, but not disintegrated.
5. Serve over boiled rice and sprinkle with grated cheese.
Serves 4

VEGETARIAN SPAGHETTI BOLOGNAISE

1 medium onion, diced
1 clove garlic, crushed
1 tablespoon polyunsaturated oil
$\frac{1}{2}$ cup dry textured vegetable protein
mince (T.V.P.) (soak in 1 cup of
water for at least 15 minutes)
$\frac{1}{2}$ teaspoon mixed herbs
Pepper
2 medium tomatoes
1 cup water
$\frac{1}{3}$ cup tomato paste

Method
1. Fry onion with garlic in oil until golden and tender.
2. Drain excess water from mince.
3. Add mince with herbs and pepper to onions and fry until golden brown.
4. Peel and roughly chop tomatoes and add to mince mixture.
5. Blend water and tomato paste and add to mince mixture. Mix well and allow to simmer gently, covered, for 45 minutes.
6. Serve on a bed of spaghetti.
Serves 4

MACARONI AND VEGETABLE BAKE

1 cup dry macaroni

1 medium onion

2 celery sticks

$\frac{1}{4}$ red capsicum

2 tablespoons flour

Pinch mustard

Pinch cayenne pepper

Pepper

2 tablespoons polyunsaturated margarine

1 cup milk

1 cup grated tasty cheese

2 small tomatoes

Method

1. Bring a saucepan of water to the boil. Add macaroni and boil until tender (about 15–20 minutes).

2. Dice onion, celery and capsicum and boil together for 5 minutes.

3. Mix flour with mustard, cayenne pepper and pepper.

4. Melt margarine in a saucepan, add flour mixture and cook over a low heat for 1 minute.

5. Gradually stir in milk and stir continuously until mixture boils and thickens.

6. Add cooked macaroni and half the cheese.

7. Lightly grease an ovenproof dish and layer with macaroni mixture, vegetables and thinly sliced tomato until all mixtures are used.

8. Sprinkle with remaining cheese and bake at 190°C (375°F) for 20–25 minutes or until golden brown.

Serves 4–6

THUNDER AND LIGHTNING

150 g dry macaroni

1 small onion, chopped

1 tablespoon margarine

200 g sliced mushrooms

250 g cooked chickpeas (or use canned)

$\frac{1}{2}$ cup grated cheese

Method

1. Boil macaroni till cooked.

2. Fry onion in margarine till soft.

3. Add mushrooms and cook slowly till mushroom juices start to run.

4. Mix in chickpeas and cook for further 5 minutes.

5. Mix with pasta.

6. Sprinkle with cheese.

Serves 4

SPINACH LASAGNE

6 sheets lasagne
1 medium onion
3 medium mushrooms
1 tablespoon polyunsaturated
   margarine
2 cloves garlic
2 medium tomatoes
$\frac{1}{3}$ cup tomato paste
Pepper
1 cup water (approx.)
$1\frac{1}{2}$ cups shredded spinach
$1\frac{1}{2}$ cups grated tasty cheese

Sauce

2 tablespoons polyunsaturated
   margarine
2 tablespoons flour
1 cup milk
$\frac{1}{2}$ cup grated tasty cheese

Method

1. Bring a large saucepan of water with a little oil in it to the boil and cook lasagne sheets, separately, for about 10–15 minutes. Drain well.

2. Finely chop onion and mushrooms and sauté in margarine with crushed garlic for a few minutes.

3. Peel and chop tomatoes and add to onion mixture with tomato paste and pepper.

4. Add just enough water to cover mixture and cook for 15 minutes.

5. Melt margarine for sauce. Stir in flour and cook over a low heat for 1 minute. Gradually stir in milk, stirring constantly until mixture boils and thickens.

6. Stir in $\frac{1}{2}$ cup grated cheese.

7. Lightly grease a baking dish and line with just enough lasagne sheets. Top with some tomato and onion mixture, then a layer of spinach, followed by white sauce sprinkled with grated cheese. Continue in this fashion until all mixtures are used. Sprinkle with grated cheese on top.

8. Bake at 190°C (375°F) for 20–30 minutes or until golden brown.
Serves 4

NOODLES WITH WALNUTS

450 g tagliatelle
100 g ground walnuts
450 g ricotta cheese
100 g parmesan cheese
1 clove garlic (optional)

Method

1. Boil pasta till soft.

2. Meanwhile mix nuts, cheeses and crushed garlic (if used).

3. Add some of the pasta cooking liquid to this mixture to make it of pouring consistency.

4. Add hot cooked noodles, toss to coat.
Serves 4–6

STUFFED CABBAGE ROLLS

2–3 cabbage leaves
1 tablespoon polyunsaturated oil
2 small zucchini (courgettes), diced
1 medium onion, diced
1 tomato, chopped
½ teaspoon lemon juice
Pinch mixed herbs
Pepper
½ cup cooked brown rice

Sauce

2 tablespoons chopped onion
2 green capsicum rings, chopped
3 mushrooms
1 teaspoon polyunsaturated margarine
150 mL water
1 teaspoon cornflour
Pepper

Method

1. Blanch cabbage leaves in boiling water for 2–3 minutes. Remove and allow to cool.
2. Heat oil in pan and add zucchini and onion. Sauté until golden in colour and just tender.
3. Add tomato, lemon juice, herbs and pepper. Mix well and remove from heat.
4. Fold in cooked rice.
5. Carefully spoon mixture evenly into cabbage leaves.
6. Roll up tightly, making sure you enclose the edges.
7. Place closely together in a lightly oiled baking dish, pour a little water over and bake at 190°C (375°F) for 30 minutes, or until tender.
8. Melt margarine in pan and lightly sauté onion, capsicum and mushrooms.
9. Blend cornflour, pepper and water together.
10. Add to onion mixture, stirring continuously until mixture boils and thickens. Remove from heat.
11. Pour sauce over cabbage rolls and serve.
Serves 2–3

BROCCOLI AND PASTA

3 cups broccoli florets
400 g dry pasta, e.g. macaroni
1 small onion, chopped
1 tablespoon oil
1 clove garlic (optional)
1 cup grated strong cheese

Method

1. Steam broccoli till just soft.
2. Meanwhile boil pasta till *al dente.*
3. Fry onion in oil (and garlic if used) till soft.
4. Combine broccoli, pasta and onion and heat in oven at 200°C (400°F) for 5 minutes.
5. Sprinkle with cheese and serve.
Serves 4

MUSHROOM AND CREAM SAUCE FOR RICE OR SPAGHETTI

1 small onion
150 g fresh mushrooms
1 teaspoon oil or butter
1 bay leaf
150 g ricotta or cottage cheese
100 mL milk
Black pepper

Method

1. Chop onion and slice mushrooms.
2. Heat oil or butter in saucepan with tight-fitting lid. Add onion and stir quickly until all pieces are coated with fat.
3. Turn down heat and cover pan with lid. Allow onion to cook slowly in its own steam.
4. When the onion is soft (about 5 minutes) add mushrooms and bay leaf. Cover pan again and leave to cook slowly.
5. Meanwhile, blend ricotta (or cottage) cheese with milk until smooth.
6. When mushrooms are soft cook with lid off for a minute, to evaporate as much liquid as possible.
7. Gradually add the cheese/milk mixture off the heat, stirring all the time.
8. Add black pepper and serve immediately over rice or spaghetti.
Serves 4

PEA AND CREAM SAUCE FOR RICE OR SPAGHETTI

1 small onion
1 teaspoon oil or butter
1 cup fresh or frozen peas
1 tablespoon cooking sherry or port
150 g ricotta or cottage cheese
100 mL milk
*2 tablespoons grated parmesan or
    romano cheese*

Method

1. Cook onion as in recipe for Mushroom and Cream Sauce.
2. When soft add peas. Add the sherry or port and cook peas (fresh peas will need longer cooking).
3. Meanwhile, blend milk with ricotta or cottage cheese.
4. Gradually add the milk/cheese mixture to the peas, stirring all the time.
5. Pour over cooked rice or pasta and stir in parmesan or romano cheese.
Serves 4

SALADS

BASIC SALAD

3–4 lettuce leaves
1 medium tomato
1 orange
1 pineapple ring
1 tablespoon finely chopped onion
$\frac{1}{2}$ capsicum, sliced
Small amount pineapple juice

Method
1. Line serving bowl with lettuce leaves.
2. Chop tomato, orange and pineapple.
3. Combine with all remaining ingredients and serve in lettuce leaves.
Serves 3

COTTAGE CHEESE AND DATE SALAD

1 lettuce leaf
$\frac{1}{4}$ cup cottage cheese
1 tablespoon finely chopped celery
1 teaspoon finely chopped red capsicum
1 tablespoon chopped dates

Method
1. Wash lettuce leaf and place in serving bowl.
2. Mix all remaining ingredients together and spoon into lettuce leaf.
3. Serve garnished with a capsicum ring.
Serves 1

GADO GADO

A range of steamed vegetables, about
400 g in all, e.g. green beans,
cauliflower, carrots, bean sprouts,
green capsicum strips
150 g raw cucumber strips
2 large boiled potatoes, cubed
4 hard-boiled eggs

Sauce

$1\frac{1}{2}$–2 cups milk
1 cup crunchy peanut butter
1 medium onion
1 tablespoon honey
3 tablespoons lemon juice
2 teaspoons soy sauce

Method
Arrange vegetables on serving dish with eggs.
To make sauce:
1. Boil milk.
2. Blend other ingredients in blender.
3. Add milk gradually until sauce is of a runny consistency.
4. Pour sauce over vegetables.
5. Sauce thickens on cooling.
Serves 4

TABOULEH

350 g bulgar (cracked wheat)
125 g chopped fresh parsley
50 g chopped fresh mint
1 medium onion, finely chopped
2 medium tomatoes, chopped
4 tablespoons oil (preferably olive oil)
2 tablespoons lemon juice
Ground black pepper

Method
1. Soak the bulgar in cold water for 45 minutes then squeeze out as much water as possible.
2. Mix together with the parsley, mint, onion and tomatoes.
3. Mix oil and lemon juice together and pour over tabouleh.
4. Add fresh ground pepper.
Serves 4

BREADS AND PASTRIES

WHOLEMEAL (WHOLEWHEAT) ROLLS

40 g yeast
1 cup warm water
1 teaspoon sugar
$\frac{1}{4}$ cup warm milk
$1\frac{1}{2}$ cups white flour
$1\frac{1}{2}$ cups wholemeal (wholewheat) flour

Glaze

1 egg
50 mL water
2 tablespoons sesame seeds

Method

1. Dissolve yeast in $\frac{1}{2}$ cup warm water with the sugar. Set aside in a warm place until it becomes light and fluffy. Add the warm milk.

2. Sift flours together, add the yeast mixture and mix to a smooth dough. Add the rest of the warm water, mix into dough.

3. Cover with a damp cloth and leave to double in bulk in a warm spot.

4. Punch down and knead until smooth (about 6–8 times).

5. Divide into 8–10 balls. Knead each ball lightly until round and smooth.

6. Place on a greased tray. Cover with a damp cloth and stand in a warm place until the dough doubles in bulk.

7. Mix beaten egg and water together. Glaze rolls lightly and sprinkle with sesame seeds.

8. Bake at 200°C (400°F) for approximately 15 minutes, or until rolls sound hollow when tapped.
Serves 8–10

PUMPKIN AND OAT SCONES

1 cup white self-raising flour
$\frac{1}{2}$ cup wholemeal (wholewheat) self-raising flour
$\frac{1}{2}$ cup rolled oats
2 tablespoons margarine
1 cup mashed cooked pumpkin
$\frac{1}{2}$ cup grated cheese
$\frac{1}{3}$ cup milk (approx.)
$\frac{1}{4}$ teaspoon paprika

Method
1. Sift flours together into a bowl. Add oats.
2. Rub in margarine.
3. Add mashed pumpkin, grated cheese, milk and paprika. Mix to a soft dough.
4. Place scone mix on a floured board and knead gently.
5. Press out with palm of hand until scone mix is about 3 cm thick.
6. Cut with a scone cutter and place on a greased and floured scone tray.
7. Bake at 200°C (400°F) for 10–12 minutes.
Serves 10–12

CHEESE AND ONION SCONES

1 cup self-raising flour
1 cup wholemeal (wholewheat) flour
Pinch paprika
2 tablespoons margarine
1 small onion, chopped
$\frac{1}{2}$ cup grated cheese
$\frac{1}{2}$ cup milk (approx.)

Method
1. Sift flours and paprika together into a bowl.
2. Rub in margarine until the mixture resembles fine breadcrumbs.
3. Add chopped onion and grated cheese to flour mix.
4. Gradually add milk (not all may be needed) and mix with a knife until it forms a soft dough.
5. Turn onto a floured board and knead till smooth.
6. Flatten scone mix with palm of hand until about 3 cm thick.
7. Cut with a scone cutter. Glaze with extra milk.
8. Place on a greased and floured scone tray.
9. Bake at 220°C (425°F) for 10–12 minutes or until brown.
Serves 10–12

HERB BREAD

20 g yeast

$\frac{1}{2}$ cup warm water

$\frac{1}{2}$ cup warm milk

2 teaspoons sugar

1 tablespoon butter

$\frac{1}{2}$ teaspoon marjoram

$\frac{1}{2}$ teaspoon dill

$\frac{1}{4}$ teaspoon mixed herbs

1 teaspoon chives

$\frac{1}{2}$ teaspoon thyme

$1\frac{1}{2}$ cups wholemeal (wholewheat) flour

$1\frac{1}{2}$ cups white flour

1 beaten egg

50 mL water

2 tablespoons sesame seeds

Method

1. Add yeast to warm water and let stand in a warm place until light and fluffy.

2. Add warm milk, sugar, butter and herbs.

3. Add yeast mixture to sifted flours and mix to a soft dough.

4. Cover dough with a damp cloth and let stand in a warm place until dough doubles in size.

5. Punch down and turn dough onto a lightly floured board and knead lightly until smooth.

6. Roll into 2 small loaf shapes. Glaze with egg and 50 mL of water mixed together. Sprinkle with sesame seeds.

7. Put into two greased and floured loaf tins. Cover with a damp cloth and leave in a warm place to double in bulk.

8. Bake at 200°C (400°F) for 20–25 minutes, or until bread sounds hollow when tapped.

Makes 2 small loaves

SPINACH AND RICOTTA ENVELOPES

20 g dried yeast

$\frac{1}{4}$ cup warm milk

1 teaspoon sugar

2 cups flour

1 cup spinach, cooked and chopped

$\frac{3}{4}$ cup grated tasty cheese

$\frac{1}{4}$ cup ricotta cheese

Pinch pepper

$\frac{1}{4}$ teaspoon oregano

1 teaspoon lemon juice

1 beaten egg

50 mL water

2 tablespoons parmesan cheese

Method

1. Mix yeast with warm milk and sugar. Let stand in a warm place until mixture becomes light and fluffy.

2. Sift flour and add yeast mixture. Mix to a soft dough, cover with a damp cloth and let double in bulk.

3. Cook, drain and chop the spinach finely. Mix spinach with tasty and ricotta cheeses, pepper, oregano and lemon juice.

4. Punch down dough and knead until smooth. Roll out and cut into 10-cm squares.

5. Place a tablespoon of spinach mixture in the centre of each square.

6. Pull the corners into the centre.

7. Place on a greased tray. Glaze with egg mixed with water.

8. Sprinkle with parmesan cheese. Cover with a damp cloth and let double in size in a warm spot.

9. Place in the oven at 200°C (400°F) and bake until golden brown (about 15–20 minutes).

Serves 6–8

ZUCCHINI (COURGETTE) AND WALNUT LOAF

2 medium zucchini

$\frac{1}{2}$ cup walnuts

2 cups wholemeal (wholewheat) flour

2 cups white flour

$\frac{1}{4}$ teaspoon paprika

$\frac{1}{4}$ teaspoon oregano

1 tablespoon margarine

25 g dried yeast

1 teaspoon sugar

140 mL lukewarm water

Method

1. Wash and grate zucchini. Chop walnuts.

2. Sift dry ingredients together. Rub in margarine.

3. Dissolve yeast and sugar in $\frac{1}{4}$ cup of the warm water and let stand until it becomes light and fluffy.

4. Pour yeast mixture into dry ingredients and mix well. Add remaining water gradually, mixing well.

5. Fold in zucchini and walnuts. Cover dough with a damp cloth and let stand in a warm place until it doubles in bulk.

6. Punch dough down and knead until smooth, about 6–8 times.

7. Separate dough into two. Roll out each half into an oblong shape and roll up and place in a greased loaf tin.

8. Cover with a damp cloth and stand in a warm place until it doubles in bulk.

9. Bake at 200°C (400°F) for about 30 minutes, or until it sounds hollow when tapped.

Makes 2 loaves

FRUIT AND NUT SCROLLS

30 g dried yeast

1 cup slightly warm milk

2 tablespoons white sugar

2 cups flour

$\frac{1}{4}$ teaspoon mixed spice

2 tablespoons butter

$\frac{1}{4}$ cup brown sugar

$\frac{1}{4}$ teaspoon cinnamon

$\frac{1}{4}$ cup sultanas

$\frac{1}{4}$ cup raisins

$\frac{1}{4}$ cup dates

$\frac{1}{2}$ cup mixed nuts

Method

1. Dissolve yeast in warm milk and sugar. Stand in a warm place until it becomes frothy.

2. Sift flour and spice into a bowl. Add yeast mixture and mix to a soft dough.

3. Cover with a damp cloth and let stand in a warm place until it doubles in bulk.

4. Melt butter, add brown sugar and cinnamon. Stir through fruit and chopped mixed nuts.

5. Remove yeast dough and knead lightly on a floured board.

6. Roll out into an oblong shape. Spread fruit mixture over top and roll up.

7. Cut roll into 3-cm rounds and place in a greased round cake tin side up.

8. Cover with a damp cloth and let stand until dough doubles in size again.

9. Bake at 200°C (400°F) until golden brown, about 20 minutes. (The scrolls can be glazed before baking with a mixture of hot water and sugar.)

Serves 6–8

FRUIT AND MALT LOAF

2 cups self-raising flour

$\frac{1}{2}$ teaspoon bicarbonate of soda

$\frac{3}{4}$ cup sultanas

3 tablespoons golden syrup

3 tablespoons malt extract

150 mL milk

1 egg, beaten

Method

1. Sift flour and bicarbonate of soda into a bowl. Add sultanas.

2. Melt golden syrup and malt extract over bowl of hot water. Gradually blend in milk.

3. Make a well in the dry ingredients, pour in the syrup mixture and beaten egg.

4. Beat well until mixture has a smooth consistency.

5. Pour into a well-greased loaf tin.

6. Bake in the centre of the oven for 50–60 minutes at 180°C (350°F).

Makes 1 loaf

BANANA AND HONEY SCONES

1 cup wholemeal (wholewheat) self-
    raising flour
1 cup white self-raising flour
Pinch cinnamon
2 tablespoons margarine
2 tablespoons honey
$\frac{1}{2}$ cup milk
2 medium-sized ripe bananas

Method
1. Sift flours and cinnamon together into a bowl.
2. Rub in margarine until mixture resembles fine breadcrumbs.
3. Mix honey with milk.
4. Mash bananas.
5. Fold bananas into flour mixture and gradually add the milk, mixing through with a knife until a soft dough is formed. All the liquid may not be needed.
6. Turn scone mix onto a floured board and knead gently till smooth.
7. Flatten scone mix out with palm of hand until about 3 cm thick.
8. Cut with scone cutter and place on a greased and floured scone tray.
9. Bake at 230°C (450°F) for 10–12 minutes or until brown.
Serves 10–12

BIBLIOGRAPHY

American Dietetic Association,
"Position paper on the vegetarian approach to eating",
Journal of the American Dietetic Association 77, 1980, p. 61.

Lappe-Moore, F.,
Diets for a Small Planet,
Ballantine Books Inc., New York, 1971.

McLean, Paula,
Good Food for Babies and Toddlers,
Angus & Robertson, Sydney, 1979.

Vyhmeister, I., Register, V., & Sonnenberg, M.,
"Safe Vegetarian Diets for Children",
Pediatric Clinic of North America 24, 1977, p. 203.

INDEX TO RECIPES